The Settling

Vivienne Hanna-Artt

The Settling

Rainbow Valley Books

First Published in 2022 by Rainbow Valley Books
Bula Matra House
205 Sanderstead Road
South Croydon
CR2 0PH

www.rainbowvalleybooks.com

fff

Printed and bound by CPI Group (UK) Ltd

Contents

About the Author

Vivienne Hanna-Artt was born and grew up in Northern Ireland. She has lived and worked in England for most of her adult life. Her childhood years in Northern Ireland were formative ones to which can be traced the beginnings of her love of story and the music and imagery of poetry. She began writing in her teens, developing her interest at Queen's University, Belfast.

Vivienne is passionate about poetry and values it as a source of truth, joy and vision. She has had poems published in several poetry collections and literary journals and has taken part in numerous poetry readings.

This collection: *The Settling,* includes new poetry and a number of vignettes. Her first collection *Blue Moon Rising* was published in 2016.

Among her other interests are Art and Art History, languages and travel. She has lived for a time in France and has travelled extensively in Italy and Greece.

Acknowledgements

My thanks are due to Michael Round for the setting and publication of this book and the cover design. I would also like to thank Dorothy Nelson for her pragmatic encouragement during the preparation of this material for publication.

It is fitting that I should acknowledge the part played by all of those who have read or have listened to my poetry and made a connection.

Finally, I wish to express my deeply-felt gratitude to the late Elizabeth Burns, poet, for her unique brand of teaching and inspiration, the positive effect of which I still feel today.

In memory of Rosemary
my sister

The Settling

Free Fall

Weightless now, I see my feet
resting on two thousand leaps
of boundless, sapphire sky.
Wind cuffs my cheek
and roughly tugs at hair.
Alps are diamonds uncut
in seams of scintillating snow,
and I, enthroned in space,
am free as Zeus, complete as poetry
and more.

Roots

In February's aluminium light,
I see a sprawl of winter green:
gaunt shrubs, their scrawny shoulders set
against a tossing wind and sheets of rain.
I think I see the garden shift,
and in its stead
a phantasmagoria of places
which hold me, draw me back again:

The shady valley of the River Lot,
its hillside villages like cataracts of honey stone.
They sweep to meadows forested with maize
which clings to rich, alluvial soil with roots
like naked toes. I see the push
of smooth, wide waters, bridges, hollyhocks,
swallows doing kamikaze dives for midges,
hear the heavy hush of long hot afternoons.

That square in Rome that overflowed
with market sounds and smells:
beads, bangles, pots and pans,
bannocks of rustic bread, rank cheeses,
army knives, coffee fumes, dahlias in profusion,
I, in a sunny side-street drinking *americano*
and, just for the blink of an eye, feeling Roman.

The lookout from a balcony of cliffs
with their coterie of cool umbrella pines –
here we'd stand to gaze across the bay
at Naples in its sunset livery, and hear a choir
of hillside churches announce with bells
the splendour of the evening hour.

Or Cervo, mediaeval village perched
like a nesting osprey, high above a sea
so blue and far below it seemed to stand
on tiptoe to embrace a universe of sky;
where, to climb the narrow pebbled streets
is to lose oneself over and over again
in two millennia of human time.

I am fed by roots that found a place
in foreign rock and soil.

In the Beginning

I was all of five and a half when I started school. Memories of that time are fragmented rather than faint. I do not recall arriving at the school, though I do remember that the building had two entrances – one clearly marked 'Girls', the other 'Boys'.

I presume we entered through the former, my father and I, and he led me by the hand along the corridor, then to the first classroom on the elbow of the T-junction. There, we met Miss Ramsey, the teacher of Infants' Class – or Baby Infants, to give it its tautological title. I was, at that time, unaware that Miss Ramsey taught children of various degrees of newness in her bright and cheery classroom. She was expecting us.

Miss Ramsey was an energetic little woman who possessed all the liveliness of a small, perky bird – more forthcoming than a wren, less restless than a blue-tit, more like a sagacious robin with an all-seeing eye. Her classroom was quietly bursting with children seated in twos at small wooden desks. Such were Miss Ramsey's strong, human qualities that I offered no resistance and felt little pain when my father handed me over.

Of the year or so that I spent in Miss Ramsey's class little stands out in hard relief. It was simply a happy time. We sang jolly songs and did small sums and listened to stories. There were tiny jars of brightly coloured sweets to be won on Fridays. There were stars to collect and happy faces.

At the back of the classroom were a large doll's house and a beautiful rocking horse – a dapple grey with benign, long-suffering features and a glorious sleek, black tail. His reins were red, and, had Miss Ramsey not fixed us with her beady eye, we would have fought each other for the pleasure of rocking on his back. In the main, however, horse and house were permitted as treats to children who, in some way, had earned them.

Work and play were inseparable and indistinguishable parts of the livelong day. Work was important to me, though I did not then know it by that name. Holding a pencil, letters on a page, a word, a sentence, a colour, a phrase; a column of figures we called a sum; a house with high windows, a bright yellow sun; a horse and a dog, a pond with five ducks; a garage with cars, a wall of red bricks. I unselfconsciously enjoyed it all. So, I could tell, did Billy.

Billy was one of a pair of bright twins who are two of the few who figure as individuals in my memory. Billy was dark-haired while Bobby was very blond. For a long time, Billy and I shared a double desk, shared life. Whether this arrangement happened by accident or by design on the part of Miss Ramsey I do not know. We were inseparable. Side by side, we would write and paint and add and draw. Occasionally, I would swap him for his less academic, more amusing brother, but for a long time, Billy and I were an enduring partnership.

Very few other children stand out in my mind as rounded individuals. There was Bob at the back of the class. He was tall and pale-faced, looked perpetually lost and almost certainly was. There was Eric, the first to pass through the classroom door when the big boy from the headmaster's room rang the bell for breaks. Eric was kick and tumble, rough and raw. He rumbled with energy. He wore shabby clothes and wiped his nose on the frayed cuff of his sleeve. He ran in streets, stole apples and knew where babies came from, though I didn't believe him. He was kind and gruffly gentle, but I always pushed him away. I was somehow afraid of him.

It seems slightly odd that I should remember only boys, because there were certainly girls in this class, too. I have vague recollections of a girl called Frances. A small, dark little thing, she who, for several days after starting school, clung so desperately to her mother that she had to be taken home again. When she inevitably returned, she wept quietly for hours, day in and day out. Why she did this was a complete mystery to me because life was good. In fact, events conspired only once to blot my otherwise happy existence.

It was a cold March day with rain in the morning. At lunchtime, however, we were allowed to go out to play. I remember whirling and dancing around in the school yard when *bump!* – I slipped on a pebble and went down with a thud, landing on my bottom in a well-filled puddle. I was shocked and distraught, not to mention very uncomfortable. Someone led me, bawling and sobbing, back to the classroom, and delivered me to the teacher.

'My mummy's going to be cross!' I sobbed through spasms of tears.

Miss Ramsey was sympathetic and had a ready solution: my puddle-wet, navy-blue knickers would dry on the radiator. All I had to do was take them off! I was utterly mortified, shamed, shocked through and through. I refused point blank to be parted from my interlock knickers of navy blue.

And so, under Miss Ramsey's strong, efficient and sheltering wing we prospered. No scolding, no fuss, no confrontation, no fear. We learnt to read and write, to add and subtract, to sing and play, to compete and respect, to tell truth and obey. Good manners were expected of everyone – in the beginning.

Headmaster

His kingdom looms at corridor end.
Classrooms, as through fog, float by.
Too soon, I stand outside his door,
breathing hard,
in spite of stale carbolic fumes
rising from the cold stone floor.
Rain slaps against a window pane,
the only other sound, his voice
rumbling low – a jungle sound
rising to a roar.
I hear him tread the aisles
between long rows of big boys' desks,
hear the cane he swishes as he walks,
that stings when biting into children's flesh.
I cannot see his bulky form,
his frown, his balding head –
too young, too small.
I cannot reach the panelled glass
too high above my straining arm.
I knock on wood.
I pray he may not hear, though,
melting from my belly button in,
I knock again,
imagining his sweet, hot breath
upon my cheek, his leering grin
as he looms over me,
invites me in.

Lines

written on a train journey through Scotland
after visiting my ageing mother in Ulster

The sea recedes now, lying low,
pressed flat by leaden skies
that squat and shed
their heavy undersides
on Barrhill station petrified
at half past three.

Rivers are full-bellied, thrusting wide;
their pearly, beaded bog-water
purloins the fertile valley floor;
hills ghost their bulk, cloud-trailing,
like islands on some half-forgotten shore.
It is the fall of the wet and windy year,
a long, slow, lingering death
in the dark woods.

Back across the churning sea
I leave her to her dwindling –
my mother, breath of my life,
maker of my flesh – frail, alone,
cloistered in her narrow room
like an unhappy nun frantic for living.

Floundering in the unholy wreck
of withering cells, brain's atrophy,
they walk the phantom corridors
of no return, these work-worn women,
gaunt, somnambulant sisterhood,
hoary harem of Life-in-Death.

For you, beloved, no sun will flame
the embers of your life,
as sun will surely touch and torch
the sullen gold and bronze
of rain-glazed autumn trees
that rush my speeding window.

For now, the rivers rage and weep,
skies intone their fearful requiem.

Visiting Mrs Daly

---

*T*oday, we are going to see Mrs Daly! my mother says.

We climb into our car. I am not excited. We drive for a long time. My window is full of trees. The narrow road is a tunnel of green. The engine throbs. It makes me want to sleep.

Here we are! cries Mother. Her voice is happy. I watch as she opens the gate. I sit bolt upright now. I see wheel tracks in the green lane.

After the fuchsia hedge there is a small house. It has white walls and a dark green door. I hear cows mooing in the byre. There are many wooden sheds. Some are sad and broken.

Mother goes towards the green door. We crunch across the gravel. She knocks. The door is not shut. The paint has bubbles. I long to pop them but I know I must not.

I follow my mother into the house. It is very dark. I see a figure sitting near the fire. I cannot see her chair because she wears such long skirts. They are black. She has a shawl around her shoulders. Her toes peep out at me from under her hems. I do not think I like her. Everything about her is black, even the bonnet hiding her wispy hair, even the wrinkles in her pale skin. Her eyes are black as coal and they burn into mine.

And this is Evelyn. My! Hasn't she grown!

That is what they all say. She puts out her hand to me. I do not want to take it, but I do. It is very cold.

Mother and Mrs Daly talk. I sit on a three-legged stool. It is just my size. The fire crackles and spits. I watch the flames. They leap at the big black kettle that dangles from a hook. The chimney is so huge. It is a cave, a big black throat. I smell the smoke from the turf. It curls and twists in my nose.

The room is dark. I don't really like it, but it is happy, too. Mother and Mrs Daly laugh and the big black kettle sings.

Mother allows me to go out.

Don't wander off. And mind what you do.

I walk slowly until I reach the green door; then I burst down the yard. My feet ruffle the gravel. I leap and twirl and spin! I hear buckets clink in the shed. I see calves with pink noses. They jostle and they make a hungry din.

Ducks waddle in a line. I follow them into the orchard. The grass is long and it smells green. I stop when I see the geese. I count them. There are seven. They stretch their necks and scold me. The big one hisses and spits. I hide behind the pear tree. The bark is black and rough. The trunk reaches high above me. I look up through the branches at the blue sky.

I watch hens scratch under the hedge. They are busy. They talk and sing together as they work.

A dog barks. He is close by. When I see his chain, I feel less frightened, but I tiptoe away down the lane. The grass in the middle is soft and smooth. No one can hear me. No one can see me swing on the gate. I climb and swing for a long time. I am alone in the green bubble of the sunny afternoon.

Eve!

I jump from the top bar of the gate and race to the house. Inside, it is darker than ever.

Sit here, Evelyn. Sit and have some tea.

My teacup is pretty. It is large, with pink roses and a wiggly rim. Mother helps me to bread and butter. The butter is soft and very yellow. Mrs Daly has not moved. She sits with her cup on her lap. I want to ask her for some jam but I know I must not.

After tea, we prepare to leave.

Say goodbye to Mrs Daly, Eve.

Once more I approach her chair. She takes my hand again and holds it while she says goodbye to Mother. I can feel the bones of her cold fingers. I watch an eddy of smoke puff out from the turf in the fireplace.

A bluebottle buzzes somewhere behind the thin curtain on the kitchen window. I feel my hand grow cramped and cold in hers. It is a long wait, but I do not fidget.

The Settling

The afternoon
is framed by four white walls,
a table looking out on a grey garden,
a pen and a murmuration of words
that swarm in the air, drifting
and suddenly turning;
then, catching the glint from
a shaft of light,
they shine and settle.

Tulip

I remember only
an afternoon of sun, and lilac
heady by the whitewashed wall.
Over my shoulder

my shadow – not quite black
but dark as indigo – and
my little sister, teetering, inquisitive
as a new-born in the lambing shed.

We idle down the garden path,
through new grass speckled with daisies.

At the flower bed she stops, forefinger
arrowed, eyes round and deep as wells.
I follow their intense trajectory.
I see the tulip – egg-yolk yellow,

petals folded still, like wings,
but ready for the opening.

I see her hunker down, sun-bronzed knees
against the milky whiteness
of her muslin dress, head heavy
with curls the colour of pale corn.

I hesitate. Too late, I hear
the snap of hollow stem,
and smell the filmy, glutinous sap,
slippery between her puzzled fingers.

Lady in a Straw Hat

A unt Henrietta was something of an enigma. She was my great aunt, my grandmother's older sister. However, it is difficult to imagine anyone more unlike my lovely little dumpling of a grandma whom I rarely saw without an apron tied firmly round her ample waist.

To us children, Aunt Henrietta was like an elegant porcelain doll. She floated in and out of our existence, unlooked for and unmissed. She used to come to stay with my grandmother for a couple of weeks at a time, often walking the five or six miles in her fashionable, raised-heel shoes. Ostensibly, this was 'to give her a break', but I'd overheard the grown-ups say how my grandmother would 'rescue' her sister, not infrequently, from the impatience of Aunt Henrietta's own daughter, Louisa, with whom she had gone to live.

Our great-aunt would, on these occasions, materialize in my grandmother's house like a carefully wrapped parcel sent by special delivery. She would arrive dressed in her Sunday best from head to toe. She loved clothes passionately and had a reputation for being very vain. A little lady with pretensions to grandeur, she was erect and slight of build, with a perennial girlish innocence in her bearing. Her skin had a delicate, translucent quality and her fingers were long and slender. However, in unguarded moments, when vanity failed her, her shoulders would slump, particularly as the years began to take their toll.

She was always immaculately dressed, even in the house, and for going out she wore a suit in smart navy, with a veiled straw hat to match. Her hair was silver, quaintly groomed, while her hands with the long, slim fingers were delicately covered in fine, lace-edged gloves. An elegant handbag hung from her arm – though none of us ever saw it open.

Her greatest passion was shoes – new and shiny, pointy-toed, buttoned or buckled, they were her pride and joy. She took them very seriously. So much so that her nieces – my aunts – used to joke and say that if Aunt Henrietta's little toe happened to be too long or too big for a pair of new shoes which she fancied, she'd have the shoes and cut off the toe to make the shoes fit! In the beginning, we youngsters believed this story, and we would surreptitiously glance at Aunt Henrietta's feet for signs of tell-tale, oozing blood. We never saw any and presumed that Aunt Henrietta's vanity felt no pain.

Apparently, her vanity was no quirk of old age. The story was told that, when Aunt Henrietta and my grandmother were younger women, someone bought my grandmother a handsome hat. Unable to resist, Aunt Henrietta took a shine to it. She removed her own, settled my grandmother's hat on her head and said, 'It really suits me, this hat. Here, you have mine!'

Though they were quite fond of her, my mother and her sisters resented their aunt's self-centred disposition. They felt that she put upon my grandmother, and so I got to thinking that she was, in some way, less innocent than she looked. She would sit sedately in the big armchair by the hearth, having removed the pearl hatpins and the hat, and having tucked her dainty feet neatly together under the folds of her long skirt. And Granny, my aunts said, would then wait on her hand and foot.

We children, in so far as we thought about her at all, never quite knew what to make of her. She said little, and my grandmother's busy household of sons and daughters and grandchildren churned and whirled around her. She would occasionally converse with my sister and me – saying little, inconsequential, now-forgotten things in a soft and wistful voice. She puzzled me. Was she more cunning than the sweet old lady she seemed? Or was she lonely, frightened, lost, unwanted? I remember watching her one day, on her cushioned throne by the hearth. She sat, unguarded, hunched a little, the knuckles of her blue-veined hand white as bone china on the arm of the chair, her head nodding gently back and forth. A dark feeling seemed to bruise my childish consciousness and I looked away.

Sometime later, we were surprised to learn that Aunt Henrietta had taken up residence in a little white cottage along a green lane on the other side of my grandmother's village. I remember going to visit her there one afternoon in a summer when the days were long and sunny and safe. I took my little sister by the hand and we trekked the three miles from my grandmother's house, turning right under the shady beech trees and up the lane. The tiny house seemed deserted, but Aunt Henrietta had heard the garden gate creak and there she was, standing in the overgrown grass, arms outstretched to greet us. She made us tea, with slices of bread and butter spread with her recently made strawberry jam.

Aunt Henrietta was unable to cope for long in her little white cottage along the lane. She returned to end her days at Louisa's farm just across the county boundary from my grandmother's village. Very occasionally, my family would visit her there, crunching up the gravel lane in our little black Ford car.

The memories of these visits as events are vague. I recall only details such as the stark and unhomely kitchen, the drone of summer flies and Aunt Henrietta shuffling to and fro with white cups and plates to the table, a farm dog skulking in the background.

Aunt Henrietta did not last very long there. Gone were the hats and lace and shiny shoes and the elegant airs of a lady. She was almost beyond my grandmother's protective reach now. She would sit in her corner, largely ignored, saying nothing, nodding, thinking, thinking nothing, her face gaunt, her hair scraped back, her fingers gnarled.

Then one day she died. We were doing something else that day, and to tell the truth, even now I do not know where she is buried. In some secluded, mossy plot a few miles over the county boundary from my grandmother's village, I think.

Birth Day

The day that I was born
warlords honed their knives, loaded their guns
and black boots, marching, echoed everywhere.
The long hot summer panted for breath
and peace lay bleeding in the sun.

My grandmother's house gained quiet.
My mother, not quite a mother yet,
lay on white sheets, waiting, and watched
a butterfly stray through the open window
and the white gauze curtain flutter out
into the simple room.

Outside, the heat of summer lay heavy
on the lush grass of clover meadows;
distant thunder growled, and hazy mist
invaded far-off peaks as it drifted
in from the sea.

My grandmother prepared towels
as white as buttermilk, and placed
the rose-bud water jug
on the dresser by the porcelain bowl.
The two women waited. Calmly, I think.
I was glad of the break.
They knew all about this critical time:
Mother was next to the eldest of nine.

Children whipped hoops in the cobbled street,
a giggle of girls cooled their feet at the pump
under Old Peter Trimble's watchful eye.
The midwife, neatly wrapped in blue,
crisply measured her way.

The Bailey twins, as they larked about,
pushed Fred Little into the dam
where he nearly drowned.
In Water Ford Street an old man died.
The railway gates creaked
and swung open wide.

A coven of crows squabbled in elms
by the churchyard wall, and the belfry clock
struck three, dislodging swallows.
A train hooted, a cow in the pasture
coughed, and a dog in Byrne's yard fretted
and yowled and whimpered
all afternoon long.

Nigh on four, as the hand of the clock
edged up to the hour
I chafed the dark walls
of my rich, moist cell
and felt the deep, irresistible thrust
of life into quickening air.
A rough passage I had of it, too,
quite the wrong time of day
for such turmoil; and already
the shadows shifting on the stair.

As day passed into my first night
bomb blast rocked the distant city:
I heard the doorknocker rattle.
Grandmother lit the lamps dimly,
and humming, cradled me to her.
Mother murmured wearily
in her sleep.

Elegy of Flowers

after lines from an Aztec song

I carry them to your house on my back,
uprooted flowers.
I'm bent double with the weight of them.

Sometimes I try to leave them by the garden gate,
scratching my back on the rough bark of the post,
but they cling, stronger than ivy, stronger
than the pull of the sun.
Their roots dry in the parched air –
I feel them shrivel and shrink.
Colour fades from their tender cheeks.
They do not cry out as they wilt.
They sigh, soft as mist in the valley.
I ache to think of the dying flowers,
withered as dried tobacco leaves
or the last bloom on the stalk.

In the beginning they came, fluttering
through the mouths of winds,
rapturous, dazzling the air.
They were ours.
Together, we nourished them,
watched them take root, grow well.
That is why I carry them to your house
on my back, bent double with weariness,
but there, I feel only their heaviness,
hear silence heaped behind your door.

Grandma in the Morning Light

Catching you off guard, I watch
as you brush your river of hair.
I am entranced by the sweep
after sweep of your hand,
like arcs traced by a violin bow,
light-notes of shaken silver.
You breathe the flow of the rhythm;
your eyes have the shine of a girl.

Grandpa Drinking Tea

It is still hot in the room. The sun streams through the open window. Not a breeze ruffles the curtain.

The table is set for tea. Granny has pulled it out from the wall and raised the long leaf, then thrown the white cloth over the surface. There have been rattles in the kitchen. Cups and saucers, plates, knives and forks – all are arranged precisely.

On the table stands a mound of freshly cut bread, its crust rich brown, crisp and shiny. Beside it a plate of country butter, yellow as saffron, ridged with the markings of Granny's butter bats. Its carefully sculpted shape is sagging slightly in the heat of the room. Next to it, on a well-scrubbed board, rests a huge wedge of cheese, white, crumbling, smelling of buttermilk, churns and cows in summer meadows.

In the centre of the table stands a large bowl of Grandpa's tomatoes – red as the kiss of a ripening sun. A while ago, Granny took me to the greenhouse to help her pick them. I can still hear the snap of each one as I severed it from its stalk, still smell the rough, throaty fragrance of the ripe fruit. I know they will taste as good as they look. Grandpa grows better tomatoes than anyone else.

He is now seated at the head of the table. *Where's the tea, Sally?* he says, with just a hint of impatience, and Granny shuffles in, carrying a large old silver teapot. My sister and I hurry to squeeze behind the leaf of the table. We sit on stools. I have to take care not to dislodge the large picture of the white mare and her foal on a windswept, heathery moor. It hangs just above my head. One false move might bring it crashing to the ground.

I am the last to start eating and I munch my tomato with relish. Father butters bread for my little sister. Mother and Granny chatter on and on about people I know only by name.

And he came home quite drunk, says Granny, *and threatened to beat her to within an inch of her life. Poor Gertie. He's a terrible man is Arthur.*

Where's Fred now? asks my mother, and I am distracted by Grandpa making slurping noises at the top of the table.

Experience has taught me to make no comment, to register no surprise. When Grandpa's tea is too hot, he transfers some to his saucer and drinks it from there. I am quite horrified but I hold Grandpa in awe. Mother's stories of him taking off his belt to admonish his offspring when they were children have made quite a deep impression on me.

I avert my eyes. I carry on eating.

Red Balloon

After school,
we gathered at the tennis court
behind the village church;
a sunny afternoon, early summer.
I was ten.

We played the tennis ball
against the vestry wall
and bounced about,
whirling in the innocence
of short white tennis skirts.

Along the backs of houses: orchards,
random wood-piles, gardens gone to seed,
a cluster of long, low sheds,
noisy grunts of full-grown pigs, frequent
high-pitched, strident squeals
which magnified, bore down on us,
invaded our afternoon.

Sudden as a lightning strike, the squeals
were screams,
ripping through blue sunshine,
drowning out our will to play.

We stopped,
overwhelmed by the killing sheds,
the now relentless screams
of creatures facing knives of death,
smelling the reek, seeing the spill.

Horror grew like a red balloon
until it filled the sky.

The Wake

I remember headlamps like gun barrels
boring the massy darkness of the lane,
farmhouse windows spilling light on laurels
and forms that, dreamlike, drift across a pane.

Within, an open hearth-fire burns. The room
is filled with women making tea, the smell
of wood smoke, sorrow and the husky bloom
of white chrysanthemum and asphodel.

The parlour is a flood of candle-glow,
faded grandeur, old men spinning tales;
then, a wooden box (too narrow for a cot):
a young girl sleeps in Snow White veils.

Someone lifts me up.
Say goodbye to Jean, they urge.
My eyes absorb her waxen brow,
the jet-black satin of her gleaming hair.

Omeath

O n the far shore, some couple of miles across the water from Warrenpoint, lies the small community of Omeath.

Because Omeath was in a 'foreign country' (the Republic of Ireland), to me the place had acquired a mythical quality, for all it seemed a tiny, distant habitation far out across the water. I was still very young when my mother took me to Warrenpoint, promising me a trip to Omeath.

Warrenpoint had and still has a harbour. Somewhere in that vicinity there was a jetty, a rickety, wooden affair that rocked and trembled in response to the waves and to people's footsteps. Several boats, all brightly painted red or blue or green, lay at anchor. They seemed small, basic and, as I now know, *quite vulnerable.* I remember watching the little ferry returning from Omeath. For a long time, it seemed to make no progress at all. Then I could tell, beyond doubt, that it had left Omeath behind. It was surely coming towards us.

Suddenly, it seemed to disappear, swallowed by the waters of the lough. Terror! My tummy seemed to knot and implode. My mouth ran dry. Then, momentarily, the boat hove into view again, only to vanish quickly. This pattern repeated itself, an illusion created by the fact that, in the middle of the lough – the deepest part – the waves are bigger, stronger, rougher.

Eventually, the little boat emerged from the threatening waters. The boat was green, very much like the colour of the sea. It lurched and juddered. At the jetty, it tipped half a dozen people out, took on another human cargo, including us, and we were off! Surely, we would drown! The skipper didn't seem bothered, but perhaps he could swim.

The big waves in the middle of the lough looked angry. Our little craft pitched and plunged. I shut my eyes and held on tightly to the wooden plank on which I was wedged and prayed a desperate, childish prayer for safety. When I opened my eyes again the waves had calmed and Omeath was coming out to meet us – certainly coming closer. Relief began to loosen the grip of fear that had held me. There comes a point when the terror stops, when you believe you are going to make it safely.

We climbed out onto a wide, stone jetty. I could feel the power slowly return to my legs.

So this was Omeath! A collection of rather rickety wooden stalls strewn out along the quayside: toy boats and seaside rock, dolls and butterfly nets, spades and buckets, fishing rods and…

What's that pink stuff on a stick, Mummy? Is it cotton wool?

It's candy floss.

Can I have some?

No.

Why not?

Because it's sticky. It's spun from sugar. Come on now.

We wandered about the stalls where people spoke in voices I did not understand. Some shouted, hollered. A drunk man tried to sing. The reek of fish and chips hung in the air. We had ice cream and little iced cakes sprinkled with colours – my mother called them *hundreds and thousands*.

All the time, I am thinking. I am trying not to feel the vague prickling of disappointment, a nasty feeling like a nettle sting. There's not much here, nothing but stalls and a couple of strange-looking white houses, and one road that leads up the mountain where the sunshine is chasing the clouds. Down there, girls are giggling, eating spun sugar, wrapping it round their tongues, drawing it in and I nearly walk under a donkey watching them, wondering what it tastes like, feels like – apart from sticky.

I smell horses, a strong, sweet smell.

Come along. We'll take the jaunting car and go to Calvary. Everybody who comes to Omeath visits Calvary. This is Mother.

I knew about Calvary. Mother had told me: a big hill, three white marble crosses, a holy place. So we took the jaunting car. It was more like a jolting car. We trundled along with the horse and the man with a whip, going to Calvary. And after a wee while, there it was: three white crosses with naked men in a big garden on a green hill. The man on the biggest cross looked a bit like Jesus – but how in Heaven's name did he get from Jerusalem to Omeath?

Some part of this experience must have tired me out. I remember little else and practically nothing of the hazardous half hour voyage back across Carlingford Lough. For a while, nothing seemed to happen. Then, Omeath began to shrink and diminish; Warrenpoint grew from a nest of indistinguishable buildings to houses and palm trees and a church.

Man Sawing Wood

The saw jumped,
refusing the wood.
He leaned half his weight
on the spar,
muscles tightening
under his thin shirt.

The wood submitted.
Teeth bit in, relishing
the well-seasoned flesh.
Specks of dust spurted, leapt
from the deepening wound
to spatter the cobbles,
the toecaps of his shiny boots.
Thrust and rasp, the rhythm grew
like the pile of dust at his feet.

At the last bite
the spar split,
tumbled, smelling sweet,
on the sawdust that muffled
the ground.
He spat into the tension
of his hand and
flashed the blade
anew.

Morning Call

I turn the knob and enter.
I stop, not wishing to intrude.

She's writing Christmas cards,
hunched like an unstable arch
over the note-pad on the table.

Pen begins to scratch the surface
of the warm, heavy silence
in the littered room.

A robin scolds from the garden;
the door of a glass cabinet creaks
with weariness.

She wears a pair of girls' blue jeans
that hide the leanness of her frame.
A red pullover reflects a glow
on bloodless cheeks.

Knuckles gleam white like naked bone
as her writing hand guides the pen
slowly across the waiting page.

Silently, I tiptoe in reverse
to leave the room.
My pulse throbs, recognizing something
that I hesitate to own.

Query

Am I standing still,
looking out on the night garden?
Or am I whirling on a cooling rock
through nothingness that *Was*
before the Word was God?

The White Bed

It was so quiet in the house.
She eased open the bedroom door,
something strictly not allowed.
Her father knelt by the white bed
head bowed, not making a sound
though she knew he was crying.
The air was heavy with pennies.
It settled, paralysing the house,
even the whimpering of ghosts
downstairs.

Family Outing

The boy had looked forward to this for days. His mother had talked with excitement about the Nine Glens of Antrim that sweep down to the sea. He had helped her pack the picnic this morning while father prepared the car: his favourite ham and tomato sandwiches, fizzy lemonade that would tickle his tongue and shortbread with icing and hundreds and thousands. Yum!

He knew it would be a long way. He sat in the back of their little Ford car between his small brother and sister. Miles and miles of fields rolled by. Fields changed to moors with gorse and heather.

Eventually, the land grew higher on either side of the road. It was strange country. Sheep trotted fearlessly in front of them and leapt high banks. Sun caught the silver metal on the car, flashed brilliantly. He found himself wondering what a glen would be like, and he couldn't wait to run into the sea.

His brother and sister slept. Father and Mother chatted quietly about traffic and next week and someone called Maggie Mulgrew. His tummy began to rumble, then groan painfully.

'When will we have our picnic, Mummy? I'm beginning to die of hunger!'

'Soon, son! As soon as your father decides to stop.'

And he thought of what it would be like to faint from hunger – would it be scary?

Suddenly, sharp voices rose from the front of the car. Ugly sounds. Anger shot back and forth between his mother and father as his brother and sister slept, and their little car wound its way down the steep side of the glen. The air in the car was stuffy. His heart thumped and felt tight.

He could not see the sea at all. It did not matter now. The roof of his big day had fallen in. He felt small. Excitement had evaporated. Even though the hot words exchanged between his father and mother had ceased, the car was full of a heavy silence. He hated it. He felt awkward, cheated.

The car stopped – after a long time – in a lay-by.

'This will have to do,' Father said. 'There isn't anywhere else.' Mother said nothing.

The boy sat on the bank. The grass prickled his legs and made his sister cry. He chewed on a sandwich but found it difficult to swallow. The fizzy cream soda was flat.

'Eat up,' their mother said. 'You'll be hungry before you reach home.'

'I want to see the sea,' his sister wailed.

No one answered. She started to cry. He felt like joining her but wouldn't. He was a big boy now. He was learning fast about the dark place where the green glens of Antrim sweep down to the sea.

St Martial en Quercy

The heat is palpable.
Within the limestone wall
gravestones gleam white.
Gravel crunches silence underfoot.

The church clings fast
to the shoulder of the hill
where trees cast short shadows,
barely breathing, doorway open
like a toothless mouth.

I step down into darkness.
Coolness wraps me round
like a winding sheet.

The space is Romanesque:
a single arch astride a cave,
lit only by a spill of midday light;
a kind of sepulchre
where village people come to sit
on benches, idle now
in noonday heat;
a statue, features smoothed by time –
so old he might be Everyman asleep;
an urn of sunflowers, mute heads bowed.

I find the candelabrum,
strike a match,
fingers cupped
to shield a tender spark.

The candle flickers,
catches breath,
and reaching upward,
blooms like a golden lily
on the altar of the dark.

Field with Sally Trees

The field beyond our house was heaven
in the green of childhood springs,
at its edge a flank of sally trees
whose leaves, like coppery spearheads,
would quiver in the wind and gleam;
lords of the pasture, tall as the moon.

On a sap-sprung day, I'd climb a low bough.
I'd grab a big handful of willowy mane,
throw my leg over, dig my heels in. Then,
with back arched, knees taut as a spring,
I'd bounce up and down, though slowly at first,
until, gaining momentum, tree and branch
would capture the rhythm and gallop free –

Gallop out of the bounds of the field,
over hedges and canyons, through prairies
with bison, a forest of wolves,
across rivers and torrents, valleys, ravines –
with a wild *yee haw*, a doubling of speed,
and a wave of my challenging, hand-whittled gun
we'd rout the vile enemy, conquer the sun.

Back in the field of the sally tree,
I'd rein my steed in, dismount with a leap,
hair like a haystack, ribbons undone,
and tether my horse to the hitching post,
recover my breath, wipe sweat from my brow,
and swagger across to the house for my tea.

The Birthday Party

Once upon a time when I was a little girl I was invited to a party. It was the birthday party of my best school-friend who was called Rowena.

Very few of us children had parties in those days, but Rowena's father was rich. He owned a draper's shop, and her mum was always elegant in expensive clothes. She was a tall, slim woman with hair that sat in a neat roll on the nape of her neck. I thought her prim, but when she sent me an invitation to her daughter's party, I decided she must be a kind mum as well.

I was duly sent off in my party best, armed with a present and an admonition to behave and mind my manners. At intervals, about a dozen of us homed in on Rowena's large, suburban house with roses and an extensive lawn – a dozen of us, that is, and Maud.

Maud had been invited because she lived next door. She wasn't really one of us. She was younger. She was long-legged and skinny, with a pale face and a mop of abundantly curly, black hair. She was clever and when she spoke she sounded like an adult. She didn't quite fit in.

We played games in the garden where Rowena's dad had erected a tent, the first tent I had ever seen. Soon the activities moved indoors. We played Musical Chairs and Pass the Parcel and something called Last Man Standing, with Rowena's mum at the piano. Best of all was the spontaneous safari about the house. I have always been intrigued by the interiors of other people's homes, and this one was elegant and bright, with soft carpets that swallowed the sound of our footsteps, and velvet curtains and ornaments and pretty, frilly things.

When teatime was announced, we all lined up in the hallway. Above the chattering of hungry voices I could hear the clink of china coming from the dining room, and there was Rowena's mum carrying in the birthday cake – all pink icing and candles. Then somebody said, 'Where's Maud?'

Nobody had missed her, so nobody could remember when or where she had last been seen. Tea was suspended. The hunt was on. Somebody looked in the drawing room; a couple of us dashed upstairs. Rowena's mum looked among the coats in the cloakroom and Rowena's brother even climbed to the attic, but Maud was nowhere to be seen. The fun was turning to consternation when a triumphant voice from outside shouted, 'She's here! She's here!'

We all dashed out to the garden, including Rowena's mum and Bonnie, the maid. Danny was standing outside the tent, holding aloft the flap. Because he was speechless now – through shame or fear or delicacy – we all converged upon him, thinking perhaps he'd found Maud asleep.

Maud was not making any noise, but she wasn't asleep. There she sat in the middle of the little tent, like a diminutive desert tribesman, ankles crossed, not moving. Around her lay her booty, or should I say her spoils, including an empty box of Black Magic and a half-devoured box of Milk Tray. The other half of its contents was smeared around her face, on her polka dot skirt and even on the big floppy bow in her hair. Her eyes seemed to bulge and emit a most peculiar stare.

The rest of us were confounded. Someone ushered us back to tea. Soon, our concerns about Maud were lost in a sea of sandwiches, scones, jelly and ice-cream with frinkles , and of course, birthday cake.

Maud did not appear for tea, or, indeed, for the final stages of the party. Rumour had it that she was sick and had to go home – which was only next door, after all.

Poor Maud! We weren't sorry for her, really. Her fame as the Chocolate Guzzler spread around for a while and then fizzled out. Or did it?

To this day, when anyone mentions Maud Barnett, I see her in the twilight of a little tent, surrounded by borrowed boxes of chocolate. I hope she lived happily ever after.

When I was Twenty-two

Somewhere between Paris and Vienna,
lodging in an August meadow
of thick velvet night,
we watched glow-worms
climb the rockface of the dark.

Valley's End, Sand in Taufers

At valley's end,
where snow-capped peaks
close in to stand like sentinels,
a forest track slips through dark pines
that hint at legends, supernatural
happenings.

Today, it is a place of harmony,

of grandeur, awe, untarnished light,
where mountain river falls in leaps
and tumbles headlong, over cataracts,
tossing clouds of rainbow spray.

It pushes on, in rampant haste,

to etch its often vertical descent,
until it bursts through walls of rock
to fill a pool spread out beneath
black, spectral trees that ooze and drip.

I climb the woodland steps from fall to fall.

Fellow walkers come and go,
move quietly, like happy ghosts.
We are absorbed, it seems,
by something greater than ourselves.

I am transfused with river, rock and tree.

I choose a weathered wayside stone,
place it by a thousand others –
a community arranged in random piles
by those who walked this way before.
Like phantom towers, they grow on rocks
before the opening of a shallow cave.

I turn to leave this hallowed place.

With backward glance, I prise myself away,
hear the douse of water, hear the peace,
leave my small white stone as if to say
that I, with others, passed this way.

Summer near Loubresac

Valley beckons,
all hush and no hurry;

time for darting dragonflies,
for drifts of hollyhocks,
butterflies with liquorice wings
that swim the air's warm eddies.

Goats as brown as gingerbread
rush a hillside, udders flapping.
My footsteps tap the white-hot road,
sun nipping at my elbows.

Self-absorbed, in a grove of pines,
cicadas drum a raucous tune
while swallows toss and tumble,
looping the meadows along the stream.

Everywhere,
the pungent, energizing scent
of boxwood running wild;
the mystery of shadow.

Where the road bends east
farms shamble together,
make a hamlet green with fig trees
and flurries of rambling rose.
A dog pads to a garden gate,
mute, too drowsed to holler.

Plane trees shade the tiny square
where I rest, drinking it in.
Church sleeps like a baby.
Clock strikes four reluctantly,
then four again, wiping clean
the slate of my visit.

The Candlestick

Her eyes wandered around the tea-table. Restlessness stirred like a breeze in the pool of her young being. The adults talked in waves of conversation. Their words washed over her. She slipped from her chair.

In an instant, she stood in the tiny hall, cool and dark, sunless at this hour. She closed the door behind her, releasing the shiny brass knob a hair's breadth at a time. Usually, there was no need for this stealth. Her grandmother trusted her and tacitly allowed her to wander. Last month, she had explored and tidied the cubbyhole under the staircase.

Though she had no definite plan, she began to climb the stairs, slowly, one by one. Her footfalls on the thin carpet could not be heard, though she was concerned about the floorboards which complained at the slightest movement. At the turning, she glanced through the window at her uncle's garden. It was rampant with colour, confined on three sides by low, invisible hedges. Later, when he returned from work, he would fill her arms with a cloud of these blooms. His flowers delighted her.

Shadows lurked on the upper stairwell. The landing was darker still. Faint light filtered in from the half-open door on her right. Her grandmother's bedroom. Without going in, she knew it was neat and plain. No frills, not even on the muslin curtains at the window, not on the crocheted white counterpane. At this time of evening, the sunlight would slant through the window, giving life to the secret faces of the roses on the wallpaper. She could see them now.

Everything was still. The strident tick of her grandmother's clock measured the silence. Without seeming to make a decision, she turned to the other door. It stood slightly ajar. She pushed it open slowly with her foot, closing her eyes to shut out the creaking whine from the hinges. Then, she was in.

*

The room smelt of her uncle straight away – though she could not have explained how. It was bare, untidy, devoid of anything attractive. She moved around gingerly, stepping over tumbled shoes on the floor. The small, black fireplace looked drab. A film of dust had turned it grey. She ran her finger along the mantelpiece. It left a tiny trail. A dead spider lay on the window sill, its legs curled under its shrivelled body as though to keep warm. Light from the window was restrained by the leafy arms of a climbing rosebush that had been allowed to ramble too far.

Listening all the while for noises from downstairs, she moved about the room with the expertise of a prowler. A couple of books and a khaki kitbag lay on a deal chair. Assorted magazines were half-stacked, half-strewn on the floor. Her quick glance recognized cowboys on horseback and the smiling faces of Hollywood film stars on some of the covers. An army greatcoat lay across the foot of the narrow bed. Had this once belonged to her grandfather who had fought in the Great War?

She was thinking about this when she turned around and noticed a gun. It was almost as tall as herself.

'A rifle!' she whispered aloud, quite taken aback. 'What does he do with *that*?'

Her words fell into the silence and disappeared about the room. She was beginning to see her uncle in a different light. As her mind darted about in an effort to find an explanation for the presence of such a thing – and in a bedroom, too – she remembered stories her mother used to tell around the tea-table, stories of her youth, of how her brothers would take the dogs and go hunting. 'They'd always come back with something – rabbit, pheasant, pigeon. Your grandmother had eight mouths to feed,' she'd say.

What she saw next put to flight all thought of guns. A small, round table stood in a recess, concealed until now by a featureless tallboy. Its surface was stained with candle grease and bleached rings made by hot teacups. Right in the middle was an old-fashioned candlestick – she'd seen them in story books – which held the remains of a sickly white candle. Dribbles of wax had spewed from the wick. She leaned over and touched them. They were rigid and knobbly. In the hollow that ran around the candlestick – like a tiny moat, she thought – lay one, two, three half-smoked cigarettes. She knew lots of men who smoked. *But why does he leave half of it?* she wondered.

It was then that she noticed the box of matches. It had been there all the time, but only now did it jump into her line of vision, seeming to assert itself. She picked up one of the discarded cigarettes. She straightened it and, raising it to her nose, she sniffed it. It smelt sweet, exotic, a little musty. Still holding it, she took up the box of matches.

For a long moment, nothing happened. Silence filled the hiatus, except for the occasional scrape of the thorny rose outside the window pane.

A tremor of excitement ran through her, the thrill of secrecy, a tug of wilfulness. She took out a match and struck it. It seemed to fizz and a curl of blue smoke escaped into the stolid air of the room. She remembered what Clifford Evans had said. 'It'll make you sick! You'll puke!'

Undeterred, she put the cigarette to her mouth and carefully held the match flame close. She drew in a slow, short puff of air. She felt the cigarette respond – the merest quiver. She breathed out. A wisp of smoke escaped from her lips. She waited. No cough; no dizziness; no splutter. She was amazed. *Maybe I'm a genie...or a dragon!*

Her attempt at humour died more quickly than the match flame that had almost singed her thumb. She looked at the cigarette still smouldering in her hand. It was alive. It felt snug between her two fingers. Carefully, she extinguished it in the bowl of the grey candlestick. She felt different; she felt grown-up, but knew she was not.

Leaving Home

My father carries my belongings
to the car:
everything I think I will need
for city life.

Books in any order
fill the car's rear window shelf.

I have already taken leave
of the garden, tucked
the gurgle of the peaty stream
deep inside my head,
the larch-wood just turning gold.

My sister is inside, feeling tearful,
brother nowhere to be seen,
and our dog has skulked to the shadows
under the rhododendron tree.

Mother busies herself with normal things:
fetching eggs from the pantry,
watering geraniums
in the lean-to by the back door.
Her face is pale: cheekbones
the pallor of a waning moon
on a frosty night,
eyes shuttered with steel.

I climb into the car, speechless,
lump like a potato in my throat.

Walk in Early Spring

W e set off along the track. It threads the valley, hand in hand with railway and canal. Early daffodils whisper the tiptoeing in of spring. Sheep crop the sweetening hillside grass. High above, buzzards ride the currents, dark wings in silhouette against a periwinkle sky. The wind, when it finds us out, is keen.

Unperturbed, canal lies cosseted in banks of birch and reed. Water mirrors an enchanted world. Hazel twigs dip to kiss their own reflection. Ducks and long-necked wild geese forage in a meadow, gossiping together. An agitated moorhen chutters, threading smooth water.

Of a sudden, the sky dims. Our bright world drains of colour. Water becomes lead. Pure gold lamb's-tails turn to dross. Reflections hurry away as a vanguard of cloud muscles the sun. Flurries of downy flakes flounce and flutter. In less than the blink of a startled eye, the air is a mayhem of snow.

We turn. We keep a steady pace. Geese and mallards graze as before.

In less than the distance between two stone bridges, our world transmutes. White blobs tumble and settle. The air is big with it. Our path is white with it. It is a snow invasion. We shake it from our garments again and again. It clings to eyebrows, bamboozles vision, aims darts at our skin. We trudge and we struggle, alert to the grunt of it under our feet.

Hedges bend with it, every twig wrapped in it, branches submit to it. A lone horse stoically shelters from it; sheep disappear in it. A pheasant in woods filling up with it sounds an alarm.

Inside our snow-shells, we stiffen and chill. We endure the thrust of it, pushing still. We mutter and swear at it; hollowly laugh at it: featureless effigies ambushed by snow.

To Mary Jane, my *Other* Grandmother

The first time I saw you, I was five or six,
and you long dead,
discovered by exploring hands
that dragged you, heavy in your ornate frame,
from the soft, sweet-smelling, treasure chest
that was the wardrobe in a vacant room.

You posed in sepia, an archduchess
decked out in unbecoming hat
and high-necked, buttoned astrakhan,
not beautiful, yet handsome, statesman stern.
Your direct, honest eyes pinned me
like a startled squirrel, arms outstretched,
across the open wardrobe door.
Your lips were tight, your skin unwrinkled,
smooth but cold. You seemed like someone
from the past, quite old.

Throughout my childhood, early youth,
we'd meet again at intervals,
I, searching for a shoe or belt,
a long-lost piece of clothing or a book,
you, unframed by then,
the edges of your portrait fraying,
cracked, dried out, abused – lending
a hint of softness to your austere look.

I used to wonder, briefly, what sentiment
or thought or wisdom lurked, well hidden,
behind that penetrating stare. Your eyes –
I never knew their colour nor their tint.

No one ever fleshed me out your life;
you never seemed to wander in and out
of family stories, your silver thread unwoven
through the tapestry of springs, of harvest homes,
of funerals and weddings, of how you reared your
children, made ends meet.

When I moved away from home –
the home you came to as a bride,
where you lived, gave birth, grew old
and ultimately died three years before
my coming – you were the last thing
on my forward-looking mind.

As time soft-shoed through ensuing decades –
you in some dark, forgotten recess,
left with family bible, death insertions,
red-backed, gold-leaf Coronation book,
I on my whirligig, spinning round and round
to my own tune – I forgot you
and your sombre, haunting gaze
that I had found so difficult to own,

until this morning, in the grey dawn,
when, on descending the stair,
I glimpsed the mirror as I passed,
and found you there.

A Mustering of Shoes

The city reels, silent, tense.
Streets lie naked to the chilling air.
Normality has gone to ground.
Flower-waves wash pavements
that yesterday were stained with blood.

In this post-attack hiatus
Republique stands dumb and bare.
Nothing moves;
only a floundering *tricoleur.*
Gatherings prohibited. No one here.

Then, as the clock tower drums the hour,
an endless flow of people comes.
They do not linger, do not stay.
Each leaves a pair of shoes or boots –
defiant throngs of steadfast feet.

Everywhere, within the square,
an inland sea of shoes in pairs
stands motionless and ankle-deep,
heel to heel, cheek by jowl –
a spirit-legion's dense array.

This diverse mustering of boots and shoes
of every size and hue stands tall.
The eagle of resilience soars.
It steals the breath of gloom away.

The lion of attrition roars.

Hôtel de Toulouse

W e were relieved that we had survived the night or indeed that we had slept at all.

We quickly washed and dressed. I opened the shutters. Immediately, the roar of traffic and blue sky sunshine flooded into the fourth floor room, revealing even more distinctly the faded blanket, the patched and fraying sheets and the ample stain of coffee or wine on the dingy carpet. We hastened to get out of the room with its garish curtains that hung half off their hooks and chairs that would not tolerate being sat upon – even if we'd wanted to.

As we got out of the lift (there were no stairs that we could see) we noticed that the day was already under way. A pile of crumpled sheets lay on the lobby floor. A thick-set, middle-aged woman with lank hair and puffy ankles busied herself with brushes, casting only a disparaging look in our direction.

We proceeded to the dining-room and found a table that was bare save for a limp white cloth and a bowl of stale-looking lumpy sugar. At least, from here, we could see people passing in the street, sunshine falling a little way through the open door.

No other guests occupied the room. The space behind the bar was empty. I took in the yellowed walls, the rows of bottles jacketed in dust and posters so ancient they curled up with weariness. The floor, tiled in black and white, was so uneven that the table rocked nauseatingly. I brushed yesterday's crumbs from the cloth with the heel of my hand. The place smelt of cobwebs and withered flowers and neglect.

'Café ou thé?'

The loud croak frightened us. We both stiffened. An elderly woman had shuffled into the space behind the bar. Her face was pale and unremarkable, her hair grey with more than a hint of washed out brown. Her skirts reached down to her ankles and on top a Joseph's jacket in shades of silver, purple, black and crimson was pulled about her shoulders.

'Café ou thé?' she barked again, more loudly than before.

'Bonjour, Madame,' I ventured, choosing to conceal my surprise in politeness. 'Café, s'il vous plait.'

Madame was obviously deaf, a woman of few words. She shuffled in slippered feet over the uneven floor. We watched her slow progress from some cavern at the back with a basket of bread, then a dish of butter, making a separate journey for each. Her fingers, we saw, were embellished with rings. We watched, fascinated by her silent ritual.

'Vous êtes anglais!' she pronounced finally, as though that accounted for things at which we could only guess. Then she shuffled away, not waiting for an answer.

The bread, surprisingly fresh, cheered us up, and the taste of the bitter coffee reminded us that we were still deep in France. Our spirits rose.

We decided to linger a little after the frugal meal. We chatted about our predicament and had a quiet giggle about Madame. I was looking at nothing in particular when my eyes came to rest on a nearby table. Something moved slowly and deliberately over the empty plane of the cloth. It was black, too large for a beetle, and moved on confident legs, as though crossing familiar ground. I squirmed in disbelief, then saw that the table stood over a grid that gave way to the basement.

'Bill,' I said slowly, 'what does a cockroach look like?'

He looked at me. I looked at him. We fled.

Dust

Each time dust tickles, fretting the nose,
I think of France: of lazy summer streets
running down to the river, and sandy tracks
through stubble fields; a courtyard where
we walked, inseparable, sun-kissed;
or laughing, dashed for shelter to the
broad-leafed plane trees in the square
as rain smote the dusty flags;
and, later, sitting alone all afternoon,
on a warm step before the Madeleine,
waiting, the day you never came.
When I smell the pungent reek of dust
even now, a lifetime further on,
it seems that I am waiting still.

The Leaving

after Brigit Pegeen Kelly

My father said I could not do it,
but all night I gathered in the bundles of flax.
The meadows were still, the burn muttered
pensively. I was a girl then, single-minded,
my heart its own walled tower.
How many arms to gather a field of flax?
I had but two and a dogged will,
with the young moon that went before me
the way water runs from spring to burn,
singing under the willow trees
with a voice that seemed to speak of those
who had gathered and carried before me.
I heaved the flax sheaves into the dam,
all night up and down the dew-damp field,
all night, my arms gathering, swinging the load,
my back arched like a meadow toad,
the pale moon rising. And then,
with the sweetness of gentle rain,
out of a pearly sky the morning came,
and in my heart was a fullness, a flood
like the stream dammed up by clod and mud.
Light crept over the meadow, the sallow trees.
It silvered the flax-hole's brooding ooze,
and I could glimpse on the murky sheen
where flax sheaves lay to ret and simmer,
a glimmering world I had never seen,
or even carelessly caught in dream.
As I lowered the last sheaf into the dam
a pond skater shot to the other side;
on a blade of grass, the dawn-washed wing
of a single, sleeping dragonfly.

Dan

Holding onto the railings, he left the busy street. The cold metal numbed his bony fingers. He could hear the warning skirl of police car or ambulance in the far distance. He shivered and cuffed the beads of sweat from his brow.

Somehow, he was aware that the steep steps were slippery, greased with the damp of the late November night. Breathing heavily, he lurched down the steps, taking them one at a time. Below him, the grey bulk of St. Cuthbert's loomed out of the almost solid darkness among the leafless trees.

He thought he could remember the path that led behind the church and down through an opening in the high stone wall. Even though he hadn't eaten for hours, maybe days – he couldn't quite remember and didn't really care – he felt too nauseous to be hungry.

He was weak and he staggered. Tiny dots of spinning lights swirled somewhere behind his eyes. He tried to hurry. There would be no scavenging tonight, no counting the bright-eyed foxes.

He turned down the path by the overturned ornamental urn.

'Vandals!' he swore. 'Nothin' that a good whippin' wouldn't cure. A good whippin', I say.'

His aim was to take the path through the park by the bandstand – if he could find it in the winter dark. From there, he would drag himself to the railway bridge, even if the effort should kill him. At least, he'd find shelter in the lea of the castle rocks.

He stumbled about in the murky darkness for some time. He was scarcely conscious of the rumble of city centre traffic, peppered now and then with raucous shouts and petulant laughter, but he could smell the dank earth under the trees and the odour from the distillery. The stench hung heavily in the air and made him wretch.

Of a sudden, he felt quite dizzy. He stopped lumbering about and put out his hand to steady himself on a stone plinth. On the ground lay the vandalized urn he had seen half an hour ago.

'Aw God!' he moaned. 'It's like a bloody maze. A bloody maze, I say. It's *him*! He's out to confuse me!' A wheeze rattled through his chest.

'That big fella's worth a-watching. Worth a-watching, I say.'

His breathing was getting worse. He glanced about briefly, still clutching the rough stone plinth. A short flight of steps led upwards to a small dark area where the sparse grass rose and fell in little mounds.

'Never liked the look of him. Hope he's paid our Maisie for the geese. Shut the door, I tell ye! And lock it tight, Maisie!'

Breathless, he stopped talking. He lurched from the stone pillar and turned towards the steps. Panting, he climbed, once or twice on all fours. He made a collapsed landing into a sitting position and sat hunched for what seemed a long time.

A restless crow cawed among the twigs high above his head and somewhere, some way off, the clear throb of a clock striking the hour tolled through the foggy darkness. A faint cone of light from a streetlamp fell across the old man's knees.

'Look at the state o' them boots! Where 'ave ye been? Get 'em off! Get 'em off, I tell ye!' The voice might have been his own, might have been Maisie's. He wasn't sure.

He stooped lower. Unlacing the boots enough to allow him to remove them caused him to splutter and cough convulsively. With superhuman effort, he heaved the muddy things off, inch by inch. He placed them together, beside him on the top step. The struggle left him motionless now. The cold from the damp stone seeped into his buttocks. He could smell urine not far away in the darkness.

'Dirty buggers!' he muttered, forgetting that he was often guilty of the same indecency. 'As if the trenches weren't bad enough.'

After a while he seemed to unfold himself out of the dimness of the night. He took a few steps to the nearest grassy mound and climbed onto it, as one would when getting into bed. He stretched out. He pulled his old coat around him as tightly as he could and lay still, his head and shoulders in the shadow cast by a tall funereal angel. Only his hands gleamed pale in the pallid light from the street.

He woke to white walls and white sheets: a figure paralysed by whiteness and despair. His eyes rolled, panic-stricken, in a face the colour of a corpse. Then his cracked lips parted.

'Maisie! Maisie!' he shouted. '*Maisie*, I said! Where are ye?'

A nurse rushed in.

'What is it, Cuthbert? Lie still! Lie still!'

'Me boots, Maisie! A've lost me boots!' His voice broke down in a croak.

'Them that brought you in last night said nothin' about boots.'

'But Maisie, they was muddy! A left them at the top o' the stairs. At the top of the stairs, I tell ye.'

A racking wheeze stopped any further attempt at speech. His eyelids fluttered and remained half open, half shut.

The nurse adjusted his pillow and tidied his sheets, making him as comfortable as she could. She walked towards the door, turning on her heel to glance back at him. She saw the pain in his eyes and the bone shining palely blue through the clammy skin of his forehead.

Polly

She coloured the penumbra of my life,
this woman of the woods and lanes,
a sapling in the undergrowth of time,
a faery woman, something out of line.

Turf smoke etched dark creases
in her pale, anaemic skin.
Time leached the bluish purple
from her too-big gaberdine.

Birdlike legs stood ankle deep
in schoolboy socks and laced-up boots.
A battered beret like a giant prune
amply covered head and unkempt locks.

Her home a humble cottage –
whitewashed, lane-side; yard
with woodpile, vagrant hens, a cat,
a window-hugging rose.

Each weekday, every year,
in sunshine, sleet or squalls of rain,
she'd take the country road to town,
bag tucked firmly in the crook

of one small, bony arm. I'd see
her often as I rode from school:
a frail, undaunted blue-grey smudge
passing slowly up the hill.

I'd always stop with her and say:
Hello, Polly. Been to town again today?
We'd chat until we reached the barn
that marked the mouth of Polly's lane.

At wintry edge of early dark,
we'd see her step from frozen trees,
lugging firewood bound with rope
or hoisting something like a sack –
a tiny Herculean figure
with a mountain on her back.

Years after I had moved away,
and ceased to think of her, she died.
No one told me of her passing –
how it happened, where she lay.

On winter evenings just like these,
when shadows fall across the grass,
and darkness drains the light from homes,
I think of her. I hear the crack

of foot on seasoned tinder wood,
feel the rhythm of her easy tread
passing lightly as a sylvan sprite
among the trunks of naked trees.

Ballintoy

The lane runs briskly downhill
and, turning, drops in glides
to end on ocean's edge
at Ballintoy.

An isolated, legendary bay,
it haunts – conceals its history
of capricious rocks, Armada wrecks,
an eerie world on the wing of time,

caught fast between tempestuous seas
and stolid, unrelenting, cliffs,
aloof, unchanging – stony beach,
a scattering of rugged rocks,

a harbour bar, an elfish cove,
a dwindling track that runs due west
by cliffs and bluffs until it fails,
then boulders littering the strand.

At low tide, shining rocks of jet
are washed by foaming white cascades,
until the turning tide, in stealth,
devours off-shore isles and crags.

At the click of a sea-god's horny thumb,
the eternal land-sea battle has begun.
Atlantic billows rise and roll –
the wild-plumed horses thunder in.

The air is full of salty mist.
Kittiwakes, in a sudden wind,
whirl like petals peeled from rocks,
consumed by the tumultuous din.

Black cliffs, stout-shouldered, muscle in;
their hollow caverns bulge with brine.
Three giant off-shore stacks of rock
take on the ocean's thrusting might.

There is no ending to this play.
Primordial earth resounds to waves
that never cease to batter, pound –
and turn, in time, its rock to sand.

Short Shadows

H e free-wheeled gently down the long, steep hill, coat ends, shiny with age, spread out like landing flaps. He had done this every working day for the past forty years. Only one thing was on his mind: there were boots to be mended and shoes to be made.

His bicycle, as old as himself but more upright, bumped over the uneven ground as he neared the village that nestled in its hollow. His shoulder stabbed with a pain which he had almost grown accustomed to over the years – the pain of shrapnel embedded there, legacy of the Great War. Traynor's workshop rattled and banged as he rode past. The milky-cream ferrets fretted as usual in their cages along the allotment wall.

The afternoon shadows were short. The village square was almost deserted at this hour. Some of the debris of yesterday's livestock fair still lay around: straw and rope, a farmer's blackthorn stick, a sprawl of muck, flies buzzing. A lazy cat slept in the sun on Matt Brown's doorstep. A stray dog slunk away down the alley towards the canal. A train hooted sleepily in the cutting. A young girl in a blue dress and ribbons dawdled with an ice-cream. The man noticed without interest the youngest Hudson boy limp across the cobbles to the pump for a pail of spring water. Pedalling steadily, he quietly acknowledged the greeting from old Pat Griffin who invariably slobbered as he viewed the small world of the village from his street corner.

'It ben't a bad day, James John!' Pat called to the shoe-maker.

'Good day ta ye, Pat,' he replied laconically, and he leaned his weight on the pedals to take him up the slight incline that was Meeting House Lane.

His bicycle wobbled initially, and the worn leather bag on his handlebars swung dangerously. He did not glance at the Meeting House or at the quiet graveyard where some of his ancestors lay.

He could see the low door of his workshop now, green, sun-blistered, familiar. He slowed, threw his leg backwards over the saddle as though he were alighting from a horse and parked his bicycle against the wall beyond the red moss rose – relic of a family who used to live in the two rooms of this small and simple cottage.

With deliberation, he unhooked the bag, unbolted the door and entered the dim, sweet-smelling darkness of his workshop. He placed the bag containing his piece of bread and bottle of milk on the low wooden bench under the back window. Here, too, was the cut-out leather for a new pair of boots for a wealthy customer and a dark blue much-weathered apron. He fastened the apron around his waist, tying it carefully at the front, and seated himself on a low, four-legged stool. The sooty chimney breast yawned empty behind him. Without removing his jacket or flat cap, he took up the leather with his long artisan's fingers, reached for his awl and commenced the afternoon's work. He plied the soft hide and tools with the same nonchalant ease as he plied his fiddle at funerals and barn-dances alike. A fly buzzed lazily in the gloom and a footstep grated on the gravel just outside the open door.

Framed in the light was a figure. He leaned into the room as though he were about to step down, then hesitated. A black mongrel dog, greying with age around the jowls, lurked at his heels.

'What's yer business?' the cobbler asked, without interest.

The man took this as an invitation and stepped into the shadowy room. With the slightest turn of his head, the shoemaker took in his matted hair, his thin, unkempt beard that was stained with tobacco. His frame looked gaunt in the heavy old jacket and moleskin trousers that were obviously not his own.

'The oul' fella at the corner toul me ye could mend a boot,' the visitor ventured. 'I've only had these a year an' they fallin' apart a'ready. This un won't even keep me bare fut off the ground.'

67

The shoemaker glanced quickly at the remains of the boot on the fellow's left foot.

'It's in bad shape,' he said to the younger man.

'So's me fut,' replied the other, in an accent not of these parts.

'Where are you headin' for?' asked the shoemaker.

'Nowhere in particular,' the visitor replied. 'An' nowhere at all until me boot's mended.'

'I have to finish what I'm stitchin',' said the old man, only occasionally lifting his eye from his job to glance at the tattered leather on the feet of the stranger.

'No matter,' said the visitor. 'Time's the only thing I've got plenty of,' and taking a small shiny mouth organ from a huge pocket in the inside of his jacket, he glanced around and threw himself down on a pile of old sacks and discarded shoes. With grubby hands, he raised the organ to his mouth. He began to play quietly a lyrical and haunting tune as the older man plied his saddler's needle and thread with skill. Neither of them noticed the motes of dust dancing in the sunbeam that had begun to infiltrate the gloom. The old man laboured delicately over his last and the wanderer fretted his lilting tune.

The ballad finished, he wiped his lips on his sleeve and replaced the mouth organ in the folds of his jerkin. The old cobbler stood up, wiping his hands on his apron and proceeded to delve into a battered box a few feet from his stool. He rummaged about through the contents, watched silently by the other man, then straightened his back slowly.

'They're not a match,' he said, looking directly into the eyes of the other man, 'but they're a pair. They'll keep your bare feet off the ground a while longer. Take them and be gone. Ye've paid for them with yer tune.'

The shoemaker sat down again and prepared to resume his work. The specks of dust danced lightly in the beam of the afternoon.

Late Sunday

I arrive late Sunday, as crows return to roost.
My key turns freely, eases the familiar lock.
In your room, closed curtains wrestle down
the heavy light.

Late Sunday, I arrive as rooks return to rest.
A message on your empty table reads: *Gone home.*
Wind coughs down the chimney, wheezes out
along the grate.

Jack

I see the wall. I see the sun.
Two black birds
are sitting on the wall.
Go away, Peter. Go away, Paul.

The sun is shining
through the apple tree.
Two a penny, three a penny,
hot cross buns.
Buns for tea, muffins and honey.
Look at the dust. Dust dancing.

Dancing dust in the sun.
Bars on the window, black bars.
Black sheep, black sheep,
have you any wool.
Three bags of blackbirds
sit on a stool…

The black door is knocking.
Who goes there? Simon.
Simon Peter met a pie-man,
let me taste your ware.
The sun is dancing, Simon,
on the apple tree.

My name is Jack.
Jack is nimble, Jack is quick.
Little Jack Horner sat in a corner
eating his curds and whey.
He put in his thumb
and drew out a plum…

Jack is going to put the plum
in the orchard
through the black window
into the sun.
The sun is shining
on the apple tree.
Jack likes apples.
Jack likes the sun.

Journey into the Cold Wind

It is early morning. The sun has risen over the far hills. Birds are singing. It is late summer.

We are on a country road. I do not know how we got here, and I do not ask Boo. The rain stops. A light wind blows in from the south west. 'Bad quarter,' my father always used to say. I hear the richness of his voice. 'The wind blows wet from the south west.' I hope it does not. We put our heads down. We walk.

I think I recognize the road. Perhaps we have chosen wisely, but I cannot be sure.

On the thorn bushes, haws are blood-red. Hedges divide small pasture fields. A stone wall dwindles back to earth. We hurry. I have been away too long.

We plod on. The road is hard under our feet. Boo walks silently at my heels. The pale sun shines on the heather. Peat stacks stand black by the road's edge. A gorse bush throws back its image from a pool of ebony water. I shiver.

The road begins to twist. We increase our pace. Corner after corner; bend after bend. I need to get home. What must they make of it, my father and my mother? How could I do this, these long years of absence? Might I be too late?

We reach a fork in the road. I see the blackened gates of the old manor. They are locked and chained. The pillars are wreathed in ivy. I recognize the unicorn. My heart leaps in response. Not far to go now.

We head down the old road, avoiding the new route which slices through woodland. The pistons of my legs strain but I hurry on. At the edge of the meadow I look for the stream. Dreams of fishing for frogspawn in the marsh drift across my mind. My fingers ache to close around the jellied mass.

The stream has gone. The knobbly willow trees of my childhood have vanished. Mounds of earth where there used to be grassland; heaps of red clay, festering, wet and shiny. Grotesque machines that drone far off.

'Something's wrong here, Boo,' I say. 'These should be fields, with meadow-sweet and the hum of bees... summer cattle browsing, snoozing – all gone, Boo,' I cry. Boo says nothing. Only sighs.

My heart is thumping now; breath comes in gasps. Feet feel like blistered lead. We strive. We hurry, though hardly seeming to advance at all.

My eyes search for the grove of saplings but I see only mature trees. They are strangers. Among them, ancient plantings of Scotch pines whisper together, like old men. A black bird broods on a dead bough that shines like bone. It is a raven. Something scuttles across the road. I scarcely notice. We push our muscles now. I fight the tears that threaten.

But there! There I see the house over tops of slashed hedges. It is squat, snug on its hill. A counterpane of fields spreads out before it. But wait! It looks deserted, somehow forgotten. Panic drums in my chest. Feet grow roots of stone. But, 'Look, Boo, look! A plume of smoke! Smoke is rising from the chimney!'

We struggle on. The mouth of the lane comes to meet us. I am panting, but, 'Wait there, Boo,' I say. I point to the mossy bank shaded by larches. 'Wait there now, until I return. Sit and rest.'

The house looks sad, the windows blind. I hasten along the lane and cross the peaty waters of the burn. My breath comes faster and faster as I press up the hill. The chestnut tree still stands guard. It spreads its branches like wings over the garden gate. Our swing has gone from the great bough. A pang low in the stomach. The tree is laden with spiked nuts big as mediaeval mace-heads. I can see their rich brownness, the white of their eye, feel the smooth shine of their skin in the heart of my hand, and I realize I am breathless as I climb the brow. I hear only the whip and snap of washing on the line beyond the high hedge. No sound of voices.

I hold my breath as I reach the upper yard. Then, 'Father!' I call. 'Father, I'm home!' No answer. No one there. No car. No dog. No scratching hen, no trough, no dove. Weeds grow rank by the barn wall.

I tiptoe across the yard to the garden door and try the rusty handle. Locked fast. The suns of many summers have plumped blisters on the paint. I retreat. Reckless now, I climb on the stones of the rockery I once helped to create and peer over the tall, thick hedge. I see and hear the washing flap. The rosebush bends with blooms. Their scent flows to me on a wave of the cold wind. Mother-scent.

And there she is, crossing the flagstones bordering the lawn. She walks towards me where I stand, beyond the hedge. She is busy; she carries a basket. Her eyes are intent, as always, on her task.

'Mother!' I cry. The muscles in my neck threaten to throttle me, but, 'Mother! Mother!' I call, in a surge of joy and relief. 'It's me. I've come back. I'm home!'

She does not turn her head. She busies herself with her basket.

'Mother!' I call once more. The breath dies in my throat. I see her look straight through me, as though I am not there.

Am I a ghost? I wonder. Am I already dead? I watch, helpless, as, in her sphere, she turns away. With intent and measured pace, my mother walks towards the kitchen door.

I drop my outstretched hand, stumble from the weathered stones. My eyes burn with fire. Limbs leach life. Something severs.

Somehow, I drift back along the lane. I pass the chestnut tree. I cross the stream. The wind sighs in the high larches and a dog keens in the far distance. Only the thought of Boo keeps me going on.

I round the bend by the mossy bank and, 'Boo!' I call. 'Boo, I'm back! I'm back!'

And then I know that Boo is not here. There is only me, or what I think is me, and the wind and the ghost of a pale moon and the chill night air.

Ridley Lane

I drive away from town
taking safely
each unforgiving bend
on the road to Cocker Bar.

I stable the car in a narrow lane:
an old route that strolled through centuries
of quiet woods and pasture-land,
long, long before this sun-soaked day
that smiles in spite of death threats fired
from Covid's undercover slings.

At first the road runs down
through meadows by a silent railway line,
past hidden mounds of old munition dumps,
then through birdsong from a choir of trees,
ignoring wetland pools that seem to sleep
beneath dense scrub. Few people
ripple out of shadows hung
from leaning wayside ash and oak
and when they do: cyclist, runner,
walker with a dog in tow, I bristle,
practise 'social distancing', as though
they are unclean, a race apart, other worldlings –
not hostages holed up and raw, like me.

I walk the sunny strips in a wash of silence
twinkling with bird-calls, a meadow where
the Spring's new grass shoots tall and strong.
The air reeks of hawthorn scent so heavily
I wonder that it does not fall, shattering
the fragile globe of afternoon.

Forget-me-nots are sky-dust pooled
along the verge. Dog-daisies are summer snow
in drifts of white. Wild geese nest in a shady hollow.
A heron on an impulse flexes pterodactyl wings.

I move away,
honouring their bird-serenity.

On a rise of land across the gleaming rails,
big-uddered, blousy cows graze rich grasses
before they ripen into hay; they quite ignore
notices that warn of gas explosions
from hidden depths of landfill,
earthed away.

I scan the matted depths
of unfrequented woods,
to catch, maybe, a glimpse of fallow deer;
only the occasional hint of bluebells, late,
or in a roadside ditch or two
an incongruous tip of debris, left by humans
who think to dump their conscience
on the dead-fire side of a conniving moon;

but mostly,
I am at home here, mindful, free;
I breathe in
the muted mutter of the dozing stream,
contented sigh of barely swaying tree-tops,
the spontaneity of butterflies, the lumbering
of re-awakened bees.
Nothing threatens,
or asks me who I am or why I'm here.
I have crossed over.

Long-ago Garden

The garden lurks
in folds of time:
the yellow rose,
honey-fragrant, rich as gold;

gnarled apple trees, moss-bearded,
which, in fresh spring light,
make Sunday-teacup blooms
in china pink on white;

at summer's end,
apples large as marrows,
yellow, fleshy, juice-plumped,
lie where they fall,

half-hidden in green spires
of too-long grass,
drowsed by the hum of bees
and tipsy wasps.

We children tip-toe afternoons
looking for swifts,
or swing the overhanging boughs
of our majestic chestnut tree:
out-in, out-in, out-in,
slicing the air, pushing the edge,

dreaming of things
as yet unknown
beyond wild plum trees
and the boundary hedge.

Asine

I make my way up into the ancient acropolis of Asine on its rocky promontory, climbing among bushes and scrub.

Here, I find wilderness: rocks, bushes, thistles, sky, sun, solitude and a vast expanse of sea strewn with islands; miles of orange groves and cypress trees in the beautiful hinterland.

Peace seeps into my soul. I love being high up among the boulders, looking out. I love the sense of continuity I feel with all those who have gone before, back as far as three thousand years before Christ; perhaps beyond that. The few visible ruins of Roman and Hellenistic civilizations are small but potent reminders of ancient human settlement.

I climb at ease. I rest and climb again. I meet the Prince of Asine: a large and vividly green gecko with eyes like jewels. He is not afraid of me, nor I of him. We have time for each other.

For hours I sit on a warm rock overlooking the sea. The village of Tolo snoozes on a distant shore. In the water below me, just beyond the shoreline, is a rugged black rock that looks like a bear fishing for salmon. I become mesmerized by the motion of the waves – the continuous surge and splash of their unhurried rise and fall around the big rock. They make the grizzly appear to move his head and snap his jaw as he lunges for fish.

I hear the occasional song of a tiny bird looping in strands between bushes, watch the obsessive busy-ness of a colony of giant ants at my feet. Imperceptibly, the sun creeps further west, deepening to hyacinth the blue of the sea. A breeze brings a faint fragrance from far-off orange groves.

This is my place. Here, I am free. Here, I am. And I am not.

The Dragon-Keeper's Wife

Don't get me wrong,
I never liked the dragon much!
Ugly beast, with scales and claws,
funnels of fire that flare and blaze
from its brazen nostrils.
Why could it not be normal, ordinary,
more like other dangerous beasts?

But all the same,
when Alfonse came home that night and said:
St George has fought the dragon, Luv –
and killed him dead!
I was aggrieved.

That armoured knight on his lofty horse
is always busy prancing about, lance raised,
sticking his nose in, rescuing maidens in distress,
making a meal of it, feeding his ego,
flaunting the banner of noble prowess.

Why doesn't he do something useful – like my
Alfonse!
He's worked hard for his family all his life,
earned the king's gratitude, earned his trust.
He looked after that dragon like one of his own –
fed him and watered him, cleaned out his cave;
groomed his rough scales – even polished his claws.

I used to fear for my Alfonse, fear for his life –
but never once did the dragon give him a fright.
The day the king tethered the loyal beast,
attaching the chain to his daughter's wrist,
I knew there'd be trouble.

Though Alfonse explained
that the dragon was put at the end of the leash
to protect Princess Saba from harm or mishap
at the hands of some stranger or maverick plot,
I knew there'd be strife.

Alfonse said not.
He said that the princess with dragon attached
was happy to stroll in the garden, talk to the plants.

I knew in my heart that after a time
some knight would lust after the beautiful maiden,
and, she, bored with walking and talking to plants,
confined to the garden, with dragon, in chains,
would welcome the chance to converse with a knight,
have a bit of romance.

When St George came along
the Princess Saba was smitten at once.

That morning,
I was down at the river washing our clothes.
The sun was high, not a murmur of wind,
but every time I stopped for breath
I could hear the dragon's frantic roars,
smell the smoke of the scorching fire
that gushed from his nose.
I could hear the horse snort, feel in the earth
the pound of his hooves.
It was cataclysmic – such a commotion
that came from behind the castle wall.

We all know the outcome.

When Alfonse got there
the grass was soaked in the animal's blood,
the poor wounded dragon on his knees.
Alfonse held his enormous head, saw the pain,
the death-shadow creep across his eyes.

Princess Saba, smiling, stood by the gate,
chain in hand.
St George had won his ingenuous prize.
Poor girl! She'll learn!

Alfonse consequently lost his job.
Now I have to work twice as hard
to earn a few bob.